Rome and the Vatican

Edizioni Musei Vaticani - Ats Italia Editrice

ats italia editrice

ROMA
PER SACRAM B. PETRI SEDEM CAPVT ORBIS EFFECTA. S. LEO.

HISTORICAL BACKGROUND

The history of Rome goes back about three thousand years. It is one of the oldest and most important cities in the world. Latin, which has its origins in Rome, has dominated culture for two thousand years; law, born in Rome, has inspired Western law codes; art and Roman architectural styles have been used as models for centuries in the most advanced countries. The influence of this city, first as the centre of the Roman Empire, then as the centre of Christianity, has no equal in the history of the Western world.

Its beginnings, however, are mysterious. Its very name is an enigma: does it derive from "stroma" (city of the river), from "ruma" (an Etruscan name), or from the legendary Romulus, who might have founded the city with his brother Remus?

This much is certain: Rome originated on the Palatine Hill as a village of shepherds and farmers, and entered history around 753 BC, the traditional date of its founding. At first it was governed by seven kings: Romans and Sabines intermingled and for a few centuries the city was dominated by its neighbours, the mysterious Etruscans. The Etruscans were later chased from the city and in 509 BC the city became a Republic governed by two consuls. At first aristocratic, Republican Rome adopted a harsh form of democracy and established in 494 BC the Tribune of the People, who defended the people against abuse at the hands of those holding power. In the meantime, Rome's political importance was increasing. By 270 BC virtually the whole of Italy was under Roman dominion which very quickly extended its power beyond the boundaries of the peninsula until it became a huge empire.

Under Augustus, the first emperor, imperial Rome reached its zenith, after which started a slow decadence: corrupt emperors (Nero, Caligula, Claudius), the spread of Christianity, the very size of the Empire, the enormous costs of the armies, the pressure of the barbarians along its frontiers. In 313 AD Constantine acknowledged Christianity as a valid religion and Theodosius in 380 AD proclaimed it as the one and only religion of the Empire. Now the barbarians were closing in: first Alaric then Attila ransacked Rome which consequently was reduced to a minor city in the eastern Byzantine empire. By installing himself in St. Peter's See, the increasingly powerful Pope made Rome the centre of Christianity.

In 800 AD when the Pope crowned Charlemagne emperor of the Holy Roman Empire, it seemed as though the old grandeur was revived again. It was an illusion. Rome was to witness the long struggle between the papacy and the feudal nobles, and above all between the Pope and the Emperor (struggle for investiture) which gave her historical importance but also left her weakened.

In 1305 the Pope was forced to transfer the papal seat of Christianity to Avignon where it remained until 1367. There now followed two difficult centuries (until the imperial sack of Rome in 1527), but meanwhile the papacy was growing in power and splendour both in art and culture. Popes such as Julius II and Leo X created the great Renaissance and Baroque Rome by commissioning monuments and works of art of unusual splendour to artists such as Michelangelo, Bramante, Raphael.

The architects Bernini and Borromini built splendid palaces and churches in response to the Protestant Reformation. Baroque Rome with its fountains, gardens and palaces, is one of the highlights of Western culture. Now begins a new age: at the end of the 18th century the influence of the French Revolution made itself felt; Pius VI was deported to France and the short-lived Roman Republic was established. After the Restoration, Napoleon weakened the papacy. It resurged under Pius II who regained temporal power. Because of the Risorgimento, the Pope was once more forced to flee, and the Republic of the Mazzinian Triumvirate was established. On the 20th of September Italian troops entered Rome, thus putting an end to the temporal power of the Pope and Rome became the new capital of Italy. For half a century there was a cold war between the papacy and the Italian state, ending with the Lateran Pact in 1929 by which date Fascism had taken over. The Pope is now once more the head of Christianity and the head of the smallest state in the world: the Vatican City. Mussolini's Fascist rule tried to bring back to Rome the glories of its antique splendours by demolishing edifices, building avenues, stadiums and monuments. The war, the invasion of Rome by the Germans, the heroic resistance of the Romans and the end of the monarchy, mark the birth of the new Italian Republic. After World War II, Rome has seen: urban growth, increase in population, the years of the "Dolce Vita" (when Rome was capital of the world-renowned Italian cinema) and political problems. It is now preparing itself for the new great world event, the Jubilee of the year 2000.

THE FORA

Roman Forum

We are in the centre of ancient Rome. Here, Rome built after having dried up the marshlands its Forum where all the political, religious and commercial activities were held, between the Palatine, the Capitol and the Esquiline hills. It is not easy to move about these ruins without having some knowledge of the ten centuries of history - from the 6th century BC to the Byzantine age - only then, the monuments become meaningful. From the archaic Lapis Niger (Black Stone) to the Column of Phocas - the last monument to be built in the Forum - dating from 607 AD placed in order to celebrate the Byzantine Emperor Phocas, when rome had lost its splendor. The orators spoke from the Rostra to the romans who had to elect their authorities. The Curia, the Senate-houses and the political centre of ancient Rome, seems to have been

built for the first time by Tullus Hostilius. It was re-constructed in 52 BC, but a new one was inaugurated in 29 BC by Augustus. What we see today is the last re-construction wanted by Diocletian in 303 AD. The Curia has a magnificent interior although the present wooden ceiling is modern. It was able to seat 300 se-nators. In the Curia the so-called *Plutei of Trajan* are exhibited. They are two marble sculptured balustra-des that probably decorated the Rostra and empha-sised the merits of the Emperor Trajan. They also show how the Forum was laid out at the time.

If the Curia was the political centre of Rome, the Basilica was the place where justice was administra-ted. The typical basilica was a great rectangular room

House of the Vestals

with arcades on its sides. The Basilica Emilia is the most ancient basilica and the only one of which we have remains.

It was founded in 179 BC by the censor Aemilius Lepidus. It looks onto the Via Sacra and was originally richly decorated, but during the Middle Age, it was ransacked by the barbarians. Thanks to archaeological excavations a marble frieze of great interest for the understanding of the origins of Rome was found here.

The Basilica Giulia , built by Caesar, was also completely destroyed. The Maxentius Basilica has three aisles and is supported by massive walls instead of the usual colonnade. After the Curia and the Basilica

Temple of Saturn

Temple of Vesta   Temple of Antonius and Faustina

the temple was the most important building of the Forum. The remains of the Temple of Vesta from the end of the 2nd century BC, are entirely in brick, as is the nearby House of the Vestals; the latter is a large rectangular atrium arranged around a spacious courtyard.

Inside the round temple dedicated to Vesta was kept the sacred fire, symbol of the state, wich hadn't to burn out. In the Forum, there are the remains of the Temple of the Dioscuri, the mythical brothers Castor and Pollux, winners of the battle against the Etruscans and Latins. The temple was built in 484 BC, and then reconstructed in 117 AD, but the only three remaining pillars belong to a subsequent reconstruction done at the time of Tiberius (14-37). The Temple of Saturn is amongst the most ancient in Rome and is found at the foot of the Capitoline Hills. Its use was to keep the Public Treasury of the city. Further ahead, are the remains of a colonnade that was found a century ago, the so-called Portico of the Dei Consentes. Probably the temple was dedicated to the twelve great divinities of Olympus; inside were kept golden statues of the gods and therefore the building is considered to have been the Roman version of the Greek Pantheon. The Temple of Concord is also found in the Forum. It is an important monument built in 367 AD by Furius Camillus in order to celebrate the end of the struggles between the patricians and the plebeians; the podium has been restored many times.

After Caesar was assassinated, his body was cremated in the Forum and a pillar was built in memory of him. In 29 BC a Temple was dedicated to Caesar by Augustus, the first example of the deification of an Emperor. Today there are some remains of the podium and of the tribune in front of it.

The Temple of Antoninus and Faustina was dedicated, in 141 AD, by Antonius Pius to his wife, and, after her death, to her imperial memory. It is one of the best preserved temples thanks to the fact that it was converted into a church (now the Church of San Lorenzo in Miranda).

Placed on a high podium, it has a splendid façade with marble columns and steps.

The well preserved frieze decorated with griffins, branched candlesticks and volutes is lovely. Unusual is the *bronze door* kept in the Temple of Romolus. It was built on the Via Sacra (Holy Road) by Maxentius to honour his son who died in 309. It has an innovative structure; a circular building flanked by two rectangular rooms with apses. In the 4th century, Pope Felix IV adapted it as an atrium of the Church of Saints Cosmas and Damian. After the ancient Roman Forum it is worth visiting the later Forums, built during the era of the Emperors and therefore called Imperial Forums.

THE COLISEUM

FOR THE GLORY OF THE EMPEROR AND THE PLEASURE OF THE PEOPLE

The Coliseum is the most beautiful and majestic amphitheatre of Roman times. Its original name, Flavian Amphitheatre, commemorated the name of Vespasian who commissioned the building in 72 AD and inaugurated it by sacrificing 5000 animals. At least until 523 AD (under Theodosius reign), fights between gladiators and wild beasts were held here periodically. There is no historical evidence that Christians were martyred in the arena. Later the amphitheatre was consecrated to the Christian martyrs and this saved it from destruction, even if many stones of the façade were used for the construction of Saint Peter's. The ellipse of the Coliseum is a magnificent work of architectural engineering. Its measurements are: 188 metres on the greater axis and 156 metres on the minor axis. The façade is 48.5 metres high. The 80 arches served as an entrance to the 55000 spectators it could accommodate. The exterior travertine covered wall is divided by three orders of engaged columns: Doric, Ionic (in the middle) and Corinthian. The so-called velarium, or awning, was placed (held by poles and ropes) over the top of the building, to shelter the spectators. Elephants, lions, hippopotamuses but most of all, men, that is gladiators (chosen among slaves, prisoners or criminals), fought and died here for the vile joy of the common people, and an echo of such a massacre seems to hover among these ruins.

Forum of Caesar

The Imperial Fora

Many other Fora were built when the Roman Forum became too small for the ever increasing Roman population. Today, they are called Imperial Fora. Many of these Fora are now in ruins because during the Middle Ages they were used as quarries, using the old stones to build new buildings. Today, if you walk from the Piazza Venezia towards the Coliseum, along the via dei Fori Imperiali, you can imagine what Rome must have been like under the rule of the Emperors.

The Forum of Trajan was the last to be built; it is the most lavish and was constructed to celebrate the victory over the Dacians. The work of Apollodorus of Damascus, it is 300 metres long and 185 metres wide. The Basilica Ulpia was built here and now only four rows of columns in the central part are standing.

The Forum contained the famous Trajan Pillar which stood between the two libraries and near the Temple of the Divine Trajan. The Markets of Trajan are a wide exedra made of two semicircular floors with many shops, even on the terraces that crown the building. It is considered the most ancient Roman commercial centre remaining. Further on, we find the Forum of Caesar which was the first Imperial Forum, inaugurated in 46 B.C. At its entrance is a bronze statue of the dictator. The Temple of Venus Genitrix was built here; only three columns on the high plinth are still stan-

Trajan Forum

ding. The Forum of Caesar was built to replace the old Roman Forum and to commemorate Caesar's victory at Pharsalus. The Forum of Augustus was built in 42 AD as a commemoration of the Battle of Philippi. It is on the other side of via dei Fori Imperiali. Augustus built the Temple of Mars Ultor which is dedicated to revenging Mars; there remains today the podium, a few columns, and parts of the colonnade and exedra. The Casa dei Cavalieri di Rodi was built during the Middle Ages and has a well-preserved colonnaded atrium. There follows the remains of the Forum of Nerva in which are the so-called "colonnacce", two huge columns sustaining an entablature decorated with an elegant frieze dedicated to feminine activi-

ties. A massive basement is all that remains of the Temple of Minerva. A little further on are the ruins of the Forum of Vespasian.

After visiting the Museum of the Fora, located in a nearby convent, to the right can be admired the ruins of the Basilica of Maxentius is a large building from the 4th century AD of which only the original aisles remain. Its vaults are 25 metres high, but the highest ones (35 metres high) have collapsed. Maxentius commissioned it but it was actually finished by Constantine.

During the summertime, the Basilica hosts great musical performances. This concludes our visit to imperial Rome.

THE TRAJAN PILLAR

LIKE A FILM, THE GLORIES OF ANCIENT ROME

Perhaps, it is the most distinctive among the ancient Roman works of art. It is a story told through photograms (anticipating the advent of cinema). A spiral frieze that turns twenty-three times along the pillar's frame, and that can be read from bottom to top, from left to right.

The Trajan Pillar was once multicoloured and is composed of seventeen blocks of lunian marble.

It is forty metres high and was erected in 113 AD by the Emperor Trajan in order to celebrate his wars against the Dacians. The forty-five small windows brighten the inside where is a spiral staircase not accessible to the general public. On the top, there was a statue of Trajan but in 1587, Pope Sixtus V replaced it with one representing Saint Peter.

Arch of Settimus Severius

Some of the reliefs come from the frieze of a monument celebrating Trajan's victory over the Dacians. The seven medallions two metres in diameter on the north and south façades belonged to a pre-existent Arch dedicated to Hadrian. The statues of the eight Dacian prisoners were taken from the Trajan Forum.

In the Roman Forum is the Arch of the Emperor Septimius Severus, built in 203 AD., and also dedicated to

Arc of Titus

his children Caracalla and Geta (the name of the last was erased after Caracalla had killed him).
The Arch of Titus is simpler but more elegant; famous is the splendid internal relief showing the triumphal procession bringing the spoils of defeated Jerusalem, which include the altar of the holy temple and the seven-branched golden candlestick. The arch was built in 81 AD.

FAMOUS ROADS AND SQUARES

A journey to one of the most famous places in Rome can only start from the solemn Capitol, where was once the acropolis (the religious and political centre) of ancient Rome.

After the dark years of the barbarians, the Capitol was used as a prison during the Middle Ages. Later, thanks to Pope Paul III, in 1536 this square was entrusted to Michelangelo who designed its structure.
After the death of the artist, the square was continued by Giacomo Della Porta and Girolamo Rainaldi.

Capitol, the square of Michelangelo with the copy of the equestrian statue of the Emperor Marcus Aurelius

Three palaces mark its borderlines: Palazzo Senatorio, Palazzo Nuovo and Palazzo dei Conservatori; their façades are both harmonious and symmetrical thanks to the balustrades with statues placed over the cornices.

The geometrical quality of the square (one of the clearest spatial solutions of the Renaissance) was emphasised by the great equestrian statue of the Emperor Marcus Aurelius, while the original, after lengthy restoration, is now in the Capitoline Museums, a copy has been placed (1997) in order not to leave the square without a fundamental reference point.

The Piazza di Spagna and the Trinità dei Monti

A church, a flight of steps and a fountain form the most elegant and complex Roman urban site of the 18th century. The Church of Trinità dei Monti was started in 1502 and consecrated eighty years later, at the wish of the French kings who dedicated it to a saint dear to them, Saint Francis of Paola. Inside the church are many chapels belonging to

noble Roman families. Notice the double ramp staircase and the twin belltowers. At the beginning of the 17th century, Pietro Bernini, father of the famous Gian Lorenzo, built for Pope Urban VIII the unusual boat-shaped fountain. A century later, the third marvel was built to connect these two works of art: the Staircase of the Trinità dei Monti, a wonderful Baroque creation. Built in 1723 by the architect Francesco De Santis, it consists of a succession of ramps each made up of twelve steps (total of a hundred and thirty eight steps).

The Piazza del Popolo

There are two identical churches and an obelisk: this is the Piazza del Popolo, the apex of the so-called trident because from here originate three long and straight street: via del Babuino, where are many antique shops, which leads to Piazza di Spagna (flanked by via Margutta, a street famous for its painters); via di Ripetta and the very busy via del Corso (Stendhal defined it as "*the most beautiful of the world*").

Through the Porta del Popolo with its triumphal arch opening into the Aurelian walls, you get the impression, as you enter the square, that you are on the threshold of the most scenographic entrance to Rome. The square

slowly took its present shape through the centuries. Pope Sixtus V in 1589 had the obelisk erected at the centre. A century later Pope Alexander VII commissioned Rainaldi to build the twin symmetrical churches of Santa Maria di Montesanto and Santa Maria dei Miracoli (of the Miracles). As the space on the left was narrower, Rainaldi built a circular dome (for Santa Maria dei Miracoli) and an oval dome for the other church. But they seem the same when you look at them from the square.

The Piazza del Popolo got its larger oval shape in the 19th century thanks to the gifted architect Giuseppe Valadier, creator of the splendid gardens of the Pincio (which are slightly higher compared to the square).

Piazza Navona

Piazza Navona is a jewel of the Roman Baroque. Its name probably derives from "agone" ("nagone", "navone") that is to say "gara, gioco" ("race, game") referring to the naval battles that took place when the square had a concave bottom which was artificially flooded for naval games. The beautifully shaped square was built on the site of the Stadium of Domitian, of which it has kept the form.

The two greatest Baroque geniuses meet in Piazza Navona: Gian Lorenzo Bernini, creator of the Fountain of the Four Rivers (the Ganges, Nile, Danube and Plate), and Francesco Borromini, architect of the Church of Sant'Agnese in Agone, unusual because of its splendid concave façade (inside, a 17ᵗʰ century innovation: over the altars, instead of paintings, there are a series of *marble bas-reliefs*).

Besides the other two other fountains, that of Neptune and that of the Moro (Moor), splendid palaces adorn the square: the Palazzo Pamphili, planned by the Roman ar-

chitect Girolamo Rainaldi for the Pamphili family, patron of the entire square, and in one corner the Palazzo Braschi, built at the end of the 18th century by Cosimo Morelli.

The oldest building in the square is the Church of Nostra Signora del Sacro Cuore in front of the Palazzo Pamphili. It is a work of the 15th century that contains treasures such as: the Choir-Stall and the Chapel of St. James by Antonio da San Gallo the Younger. Nearby, in the Church of Saint Luigi dei Francesi, some of the fundamental masterpie-

ces of Italian art can be admired: the three large canvasses by Caravaggio, highest examples of painting after Michelangelo, dating from the end of the 16th century: *the Calling of St. Matthew, the Martyr-dom of Matthew and St. Mathew and the Angel*.

Caravaggio's paintings stand out for their innovative and disturbing realism, and for the unusual use of light, even in his own day, so much so that the last of these three paintings was deemed unfit for a church because St. Matthew appears as a tired old man with dirty feet.

Piazza della Minerva, small Elephant of Bernini

THE OBELISKS

SYMBOLS OF THE SUN AND IMMORTALITY

Rome, more than any other city, is full of obelisks, many of Egyptian origin. These enormous monoliths, either bare or covered in hieroglyphics, form focus points at the centre of the great squares; but they are also symbols of the sun and immortality.

There are thirteen obelisks in Rome. The most ancient and the highest (31 metres of red granite) is perhaps the Obelisk in Piazza S.Giovanni in Laterano that goes back to the 15th century BC. It was brought to Rome in 357 AD and erected here in 1587 by Pope Sixtus V, who had a fondness for these monuments. To him we owe the erection of the most celebrated Roman obelisk, that of St. Peter's Square. The Vatican's monolith made of red granite

Piazza del Popolo, Flaminius Obelisk

is 25,37 metres high and devoid of hieroglyphics. It was brought to Rome by Caligula and in 1586 Pope Sixtus V had placed it in front of the Basilica. It is said that the transporting was very difficult and required hundreds of horses and men. A year later, the same Sixtus V had another obelisk placed on the Esquiline hill, it is a bare 14,75 metres high and without hieroglyphics. The fourth Obelisk of Sixtus V is splendid and placed in the famous Piazza del Popolo. It is almost 24 metres high and has hieroglyphics from 1300 BC; it was brought to Rome at the time of Augustus in celebration of the victory over Egypt. It was then Bernini's turn to erect another two obelisks: the one in Piazza Navona (almost 17 metres high and rich in hieroglyphics) and that in Piazza Minerva, almost 5,47 metres high and supported by a small elephant (designed by Bernini). In front of the Pantheon is other obelisk, called Macuteo, only six metres high and dating from the time of Ramses II. Dating from the end of the 18th century is the Obelisk of the Quirinale (placed in 1786 it is 16,63 metres high and made of red granite) and from the same epoch the Obelisk on the Trinità dei Monti.

| Pantheon, Façade

Inside

Pantheon

Built a few years before the birth of Christ by Marcus Agrippa in honour of Augustus, it was then restructured under Hadrian (around 120 AD), the Pantheon is the most imposing and complete building surviving from antiquity. It is so well preserved because from 609 AD it was converted into a church dedicated to the Madonna and therefore cherished by the pontiffs. It is complex because it mixes varying geometrical shapes (square, sphere, cylinder) and because it fuses two architectural styles: that typical of the temples (the pronaos) and the round plan characteristic of the thermal baths. A cylindrical wall, six metres thick, supports the dome. The dome is 43,30 metres high and wide. It is the biggest vault ever made of masonry and is bigger even than St. Peter's. In the centre of the dome is an opening nine meters wide, the only source of light. Inside there is a great central niche of mauve marble, and six smaller niches around it inlayed in multicoloured marble; the interplay of their colours fill the temple with a haunting light. Many artists are buried here: Perin del Vaga, Annibale Carracci, Taddeo Zuccari and Raphael. The Pantheon also contains tombs of members of the Savoy family, King Vittorio Emanuele II and King Umberto I.

Via Condotti, in the background the staircase of Trinità dei Monti

Via Condotti and Via Veneto

The two names synonymous of elegance and high society throughout the world are via Condotti and via Veneto.

Via Condotti is at the centre of a network of streets (via Borgognona, via Mario dei Fiori, via Bocca di Leone) and is crowded with elegant boutiques, such as Ferragamo, Hèrmes, Gucci, Valentino, Versace and it is a pleasure to take a walk there especially late in the afternoon. It is usual to stop at the Caffe Greco, which is the oldest and most famous in Rome.

It was founded by a Greek in 1760 and became in the 19th century a meeting place for such illustrious men as

Via Veneto

Goethe, Stendhal, Byron, Wagner and Berlioz. This same atmosphere still survives especially in the delightful little rooms at the back.

The long and winding street that goes from the Porta Pinciana is via Vittorio Veneto, better known throughout the world as "via Veneto". Many embassies (including the American one) line the avenue as do expensive hotels and well-known cafés (such as the Café de Paris). In the sixties this avenue was, thanks to the film La Dolce Vita by Fellini, a favourite of Romans and the jet-set.

Today it has lost some of its charms, but it is pleasant to take a walk here, perhaps stopping in an out-of-the-way spot where there is a very different atmosphere: the Church of Santa Maria della Concezione, built by the Capucin friars. The crypt contains hundreds of skeletons.

THE FOUNTAINS OF ROME

THE FOUNTAINS THAT BRIGHTEN THE SQUARES AND GARDENS

Besides the great exuberant fountains, there are many secret fountains in courtyards and also small fountains at the corners of streets (especially in Trastevere) where the water spouts from lions' mouths and from

Fountain of Trevi

"mascheroni", grotesque stone masks. It seems that the ancient city had two hundred and twelve fountains. The modern ones are for the most part Baroque and identify the movement of water with the sense of life. After the Fountains in Piazza Navona (see the description of the square), the most magnificent is the Fountain of Trevi; in the centre is Oceanus' chariot shaped like a shell, drawn by sea horses led by tritons. This exuberant work of art was done by Nicola Salvi in the mid-18th century in the place where ended the ancient aqueduct of Acqua Virgo. The fountain has become famous because of the film "La Dolce Vita" in which Anita Ekberg bathes in it. It is said that whoever throws in a

Piazza di Spagna, fountain of the Barcaccia

Piazza Mattei, fountain of the Tartarughe

Piazza Barberini, Fountain of the Triton

coin with his back turned to the fountain will one day return to Rome. Another well-known fountain, at the foot of the steps of Trinità dei Monti, is the so-called Fountain of the Barcaccia because it is shaped like a half-immersed boat.

It was commissioned by Pope Urban VIII at the beginning of the 17th century and carried out by Bernini or, perhaps, his son Gian Lorenzo. The most elegant of all Roman fountains is that of the Tartarughe (Tortoises) in Piazza Mattei. It was built at the end of the 16th century on a design by Giacomo della Porta. The four bron-

Piazza della Repubblica, fountain of the Naiads

ze figures of standing youths, a foot on the head of their leading dolphin, are splendidly cast by Taddeo Landini.

The tortoises were added a century later. The fountain of the Triton executed by Bernini for Pope Urban VIII in mid-17th century, stands in Piazza Barberini. Water flows on two Tritons who held a shell in their hands. Do not miss the fountains in Piazza del Popolo, the two fountains in St. Peter's Square and that of the Naiads in Piazza della Repubblica. However, the list of fountains is never ending.

THE BRIDGES OVER THE TIBER AND CASTEL SANT'ANGELO

Many bridges cross the Tiber, some of them dating from the time of ancient Rome. The smallest is the footbridge Fabricius (62 BC), the oldest Roman bridge to have survived, still used as a link between the Tiberina island and the city, as does the Cestius bridge, restored by the Byzantines in 370 AD. The ruins of the Ponte Emilio, of which only one arcade is still standing, are very picturesque. It was the first bridge built in stone in the 2nd century

Ponte Sant'Angelo

rooms in the Castle are extremely interesting; on the third floor is the courtyard of Alexander VI which is embellished by a charming well. It is followed by the bathroom of Clement VII decorated by Giulio Romano. Not to be missed are the historical prisons, called the Mouth of Hell, where such people as Cellini, Giordano Bruno and Cagliostro were imprisoned. Finally, there is the Treasury and the beautiful Library.

TIBERINA ISLAND

Campo dei Fiori is a very popular meeting place in Rome. It is located between via Vittorio Emanuele and the Tiber. The Campo dei Fiori was not always a happy place as the statue of Giordano Bruno reminds us, for here it was that criminals were publicly executed and where the philosopher Giordano Bruno was burnt at the stake.

However, today things have considerably changed; there

is a lively market held every day. There are many other things to see in the vicinity: the old Jewish Ghetto, the Tiberina Island in the shape of a boat and dedicated by the Romans to Esculapius the god of medicine.
Today, there is a Hospital called San Giovanni di Dio on the island. There are three bridges that link the island to the city, two of which are the Ponte Fabricius (still intact) and the Ponte Rotto (an arch of the16th century is all that remains); and not far from here are the Palazzo Farnese and the Palazzo Spada

THE MUSEUMS

Rome is, above all, a city of museums and the artistic wealth collected here is quite unique.

The main museums of the capital contain, as we shall see, mainly classical antiquities; because of their size and quality this collection has no equal.

Caravaggio, the young St. John the Baptist

Capitolini Museums

These museums display the oldest collection of Roman antiquities and are located in the Piazza del Campidoglio; they were founded in 1471 by Sixtus IV. The Museo dei Conservatori is one of the museums and displays Greek and Roman sculptures. One of the most striking is *Apollo shooting an arrow* and an *Athena*, both from the 5th century BC. Quite extraordinary is the *Venus from the Esquiline* of a much later date (1st century BC). The *Head*

of Costantine, a huge bronze, is the first of sixty five busts of Roman Emperors in the collection; amongst these are Augustus, Nero, Trajan, Marcus Aurelius and Caracalla. In the Sala dei Conservatori is the admirable and famous *Capitoline Wolf*, symbol of Rome, bronze work of the 6th cen-

tury BC attributed to the followers of Vulca from Veio (who decorated the *Capitoline Jupiter*). The twins under the she-wolf are, as is well known, a 15th century addition by Antonio del Pollaiolo. In the Capitoline Museum is what is generally considered to be one of the most beautiful

Caravaggio, Fortune Teller

sculptures of antiquity: the *Dying Gladiator*, a marble copy of a bronze from Pergamum of the 3rd century BC representing a dying warrior. It was found in the Sallustian Gardens in the 16th century. Among other masterpieces is the *Capitoline Venus*, a Roman copy of an original Hellenistic work. In the Pinacoteca Capitolina is a collection of paintings from the 16th and 17th centuries: Titian, Lotto, Rubens (*Romulus and Remus* suckling the she-wolf), the splendid *Portrait of a Man* by Velázquez, *the Young St. John the Baptist* and the *Fortune Teller*, both by Caravaggio.

Roman National Museum, entrance

Roman National Museum

This museum, in an ex-convent near the Baths of Diocletian, displays a large quantity of Roman works, the most striking coming from excavations in and around Rome. Perhaps the most outstanding work is the celebrated Ludovisi Throne of the 5th century BC. Archaeologists and art historians have discussed at great length its authenticity. *The Tiber Apollo* is also exceptional; it is a copy of an original Greek work

possibly by Phidias. The *Reclining Warrior* is, however, an original bronze from the Hellenistic period: a splendid sculpture of great strength. The *Niobe from the Gardens of Sallust* is very beautiful and is one of the first examples of a female nude, a copy of a Greek work of the 5th century BC.

The most moving and compelling masterpiece is probably the Hellenistic statue call-ed the *Young Girl of Anzio*; it was discovered in a niche at Anzio in the last century.

National Museum of Villa Giulia, Sarcophagus of the married couple

National Museum of Villa Giulia

This museum is placed in a splendid 16ᵗʰ century villa that was built by Vignola for Julius II. It was founded at the end of the 19ᵗʰ century and contains an archaeological collection of pre-Roman works. The *Sarcophagus of the Married Couple* is an Etruscan sculpture in baked clay from the 6ᵗʰ century BC in which the two figures express noble serenity and elegance. The *Apollo and Herakles* is a splendid and majestic life-size sculpture; the admirable *Cistae Ficoroni* is from the 4ᵗʰ century BC.

This museum, one of the most modern and well-stocked, displays the reconstruction of a *tomb* from the necropolis of Cerveteri.

Other Museums

A complete visit of the museums in Rome would take weeks.

It is important to see the Museum of Castel Sant'Angelo (to see the *prisons* but also the Sala Paolina and *the ancient weapons*).

You should also visit the San Luca Academy Gallery (there are works of art by Raphael, Guercino and Rubens).

The Museum of Modern Art, where is a collection of Italian paintings and sculptures of the 19ᵗʰ and 20ᵗʰ centuries, also deserves a visit.

V. L'Evangelizzazione americana vista dall'Europa del sec. XVI

THE GREAT LIBRARIES

THREE MILLION YEARS OF WORDS

A third of the manuscripts preserved in the world are found in Italy and a great number of them are kept in the Roman libraries where there is a collection of millions of books both antique and rare. Among the great Roman libraries the most outstanding is the Vaticana, one of the most prestigious in the world. It was founded in 1475 in order to contain the papal archives where they are still kept today. Sixtus V had this building constructed by Domenico Fontana. It contains two million books and a further hundred and fifty thousand manuscripts housed in the basements. The main library in Rome is the

National Library Vittorio Emanuele II. It was inaugurated in 1876 and then moved to the present building in 1975; it holds five million printed documents, six thousand periodicals and five thousand manuscripts. You can also consult over sixty thousand microfilms that give you a list of what is preserved in a hundred Italian libraries. The Casanatense Library was founded by the Dominicans and during the 18th century was the leading library in Rome. It has almost four hundred thousand printed documents and six thousand five hundred manuscripts and specialises in religious culture and the 18th century. The Angelica Library was the first library opened to the public in Rome (1614); today it contains, in a splendid building two hundred thousand works and two thousand five hundred manuscripts. The Valicelliana Library is another important Roman library and founded by Saint Filippo Neri; the Lincei Library founded in 1754 has a large section on Islam and the Biblioteca Universitaria Alessandrina (1661) holds more than one million volumes on philosophy, history, literature and law.

Bernini, Rape of Proserpine

Canova, Paolina Borghese

The Borghese Gallery

The Casino Borghese stands in the beautiful park of the Villa Borghese . The country-house was planned by Ponzio in 1608 and a few years later finished by Giovanni Vasanzio. At the wish of Cardinal Scipione, nephew of Pope Paul V, the surroundings were landscaped; the building now houses the Museum, which contains the superb collection that belonged to the aforesaid cardinal.

The most famous work is the *Statue of Paolina Bonaparte*, Napoleon's sister, as Venus, admirably sculptured in the neo-classical style by Canova (1805). Sensuality has been imprisoned in the smoothest of polished marbles; Paolina posed in the nude, defying the prejudices of her age. The *David* by Bernini (1624) is a masterpiece.

David as been captured in a tense pose - very different from the statue of the same name by Michelangelo. The *Apollo and Daphne* by Bernini tells the fable from Ovid in which Daphne fleeing from Apollo is transformed into a tree.

Another masterpiece by Bernini is the *Rape of Proserpine*. The main motif lies in the differing tensions of the two bodies: Pluto is a muscular gladiator, while Proserpine is in a simple and delicate pose.

The most outstanding paintings in the Galleria Borghese are: *Sacred and Profane Love*, early work of Titian (1514). The artist's finesse is revealed rather by the splendour of the colours than by the symbolic message of the two female figures: one nude, the other dressed. The *Danae by* Correggio (1530) is an extremely sensual work of art; the *Deposition* by Raphael was inspired by an ancient sarcophagus. Finally there are the magnificent paintings by Caravaggio; Saint Jerome (1606), an excellent portrait (the horizontal layout is unusual), and the *Madonna dei Palafrenieri* painted by Caravaggio in 1605 for the church of the same name: it was refused because of its realism and found its way to the Borghese collection. Under St. Anne's gaze the Madonna, a ravishing peasant, and the Child, boldly nude, trample the snake representing the Evil One.

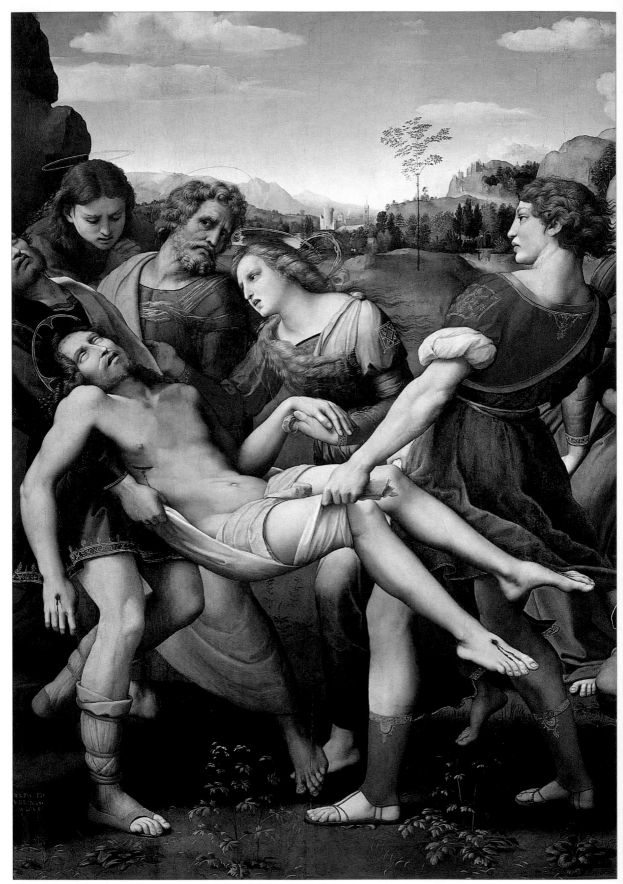

Raphael, Deposition

Caravaggio, Madonna dei Palafranieri

Titian, Sacred and Profane Love

Caravaggio, Magdalen

Caravaggio, Rest on the Flight into Egypt

The Doria Phamphilj Gallery

In the Rococo style palace of the same name, many times restructured (the façade on the Corso and that on via del Plebiscito are of the mid-18ᵗʰ century), is the splendid Gallery (still owned by the Doria Pamphilj) containing a wealth of masterpieces (including the sumptuous *Appartamenti di Rappresentanza* which can be visited). Titian's Salomé, an early work, and the *Madonna with Child* by Parmigianino. In Caravaggio's youthful work, *Rest on the Flight into Egypt*, the artist is still far from the tragic mood of his maturity. The paintings of Carracci, Savoldo and Salvator Rosa are important. Among the many works by non-Italians is a superb *portrait of Innocent X* by Velazquez (1650), some landscapes amongst which *Landscape with Dancers* by Claude Lorrain, a genuine masterpiece because of the admirable contrast between the clear sky and the dark wood. Noteworthy are also two *Busts of Innocent X* by Bernini. The entrance to the Gallery is from Piazza del Collegio Romano.

Doria Pamphili Gallery, Filippo Lippi, the Annunciation

Barberini Palace, Raphael, the Fornarina

Barberini Palace, Caravaggio, Judit and Holofernes

The Barberini Palace

Another Roman palace worth visiting for its splendour, and the collection it houses (Galleria Nazionale di Arte Antica). The palace belonged to the Barberini Family, who owned nearly all the district, and is attributed to Carlo Maderno.

Later the two great artists, Bernini and Borromini, worked on it. Bernini designed the *façade* overlooking the garden and the *staircase* with a square well; Borromini the *spiral staircase* and the *windows* of the top storey. The *frescoed ceilings* of many rooms are extremely lovely, especially the vast *Triumph of Divine Providence* by Pietro da Cortona.

Inside the Barberini Palace (since 1949 property of the Italian State) is the famous Galleria d'Arte Antica, containing works by Filippo Lippi, Lorenzo Lotto, Andrea Del Sarto, Perugino and Caravaggio. Among the non-Italian painters are Holbein and Nicolas Poussin. Probably the greatest masterpiece in the gallery is the Portrait of the *Fornarina* by Raphael in which he uses his plebeian mistress as a model (some attribute this work to Giulio Romano).

Do not miss the *Portrait of Stefano Colonna* by Bronzino. There is an admirable painting by Caravaggio *Judith and Holofernes*, which he painted during his stay in Rome under the patronage of Cardinal del Monte.

The strong contrast between light and shade and its tragic realism are typical of the artist's style and provoked great controversy.

The Spada Gallery

This Gallery is in the 16th century Palazzo Spada, which is worth visiting in itself. Today it is the seat of the State Council. The palace was restructured in the 17th century by the Spada family. The *stucco statues* of ancient Roman noblemen have been replaced recently in the niches of the façade. The perspective gallery by Borromini is superb (difficult to imagine that it is actually only nine metres long). The Gallery exhibits many important works of art especially from the 17th century: Guido Reni, Guercino and Valentin.

Finally in the *Salone delle Adunanze* is the colossal statue presumed to be of Pompey.

Palazzo Venezia, façade

The Palazzo Venezia

The Palazzo Venezia was built in the mid-15th century and is the first example of a Roman Renaissance palace although, because of its bulk and its crenelations, it brings to mind a Medieval building. Its attribution to Leon Battista Alberti is not certain.

The history of the palace is a long one: it was first the Venetian Embassy, then it became the Austrian Embassy, and was returned to Italy in 1916.

From the balcony on the first floor Benito Mussolini, Fascist dictator who had his office here from 1929 to 1943, made some of his most famous speeches.

The Museum of the same name today holds *collections of tapestries, sculptures, church silver, arms* and *pottery*. Visit the Room of the Globe where Mussolini's office was.

The Farnese Palace

It is the biggest private palace in Rome. It was built for Cardinal Farnese (who later became Pope Paul III) first by Antonio da Sangallo the younger and then by Michelangelo, who finished the upper storeys, added the entablature and part of the courtyard. The façade and the loggia giving onto via Giulia were finished by Giacomo Della Porta. Today the palace houses the French Embassy. Some of the most beautiful parts of this building are: the *façade*, which is built, so it is said, using materials from ancient Rome; the extremely elegant *courtyard* with its rows of columns, windows and arcades. Inside the palace are the *Sala dei Fasti* (with *frescoes* by Zuccari) and the *Sala delle Guardie* (with a copy of the *Farnese Hercules*, the original is in Naples). The *Gallery* was frescoed in the early 16th century by the brothers Annibale and Agostino Carraci.

THE APPIAN WAY

This is the most famous, the longest, the straightest of the old Roman roads and also the best preserved. It starts, more or less, from the Baths of Caracalla and in an almost straight line, a good ninety kilometres, joins Terracina, Capua (in Campania), then goes through Benevento until it gets to Brindisi.

It was the outlet of ancient Rome for traffic going East. It was called the "regina viarum", "queen of the roads".

Begun in 312 BC by Appius Claudius, a censor who gave it his name, it was extended to Brindisi around 190 BC. It fell into disuse at the end of the Empire, was "rediscovered" during the Renaissance but was only restored in our century.

It was built using extremely high standards of engineering (it is only in this century that this technology was rediscovered).

The Appian Way consists of four different and paved strata four metres and ten centimetres wide, sidewalks on either side, and at the time of the ancient Romans was lined with trees.

Many patrician tombs line it as it was customary then to bury the dead outside the city walls.

To whoever travels along it today the Appian Way gi-

Circus of Massenzio

ves rise to powerful pictures - of wagons, people, armies, travelling merchants - and because of the many ancient tombs, the sacredness of death.

The tomb of Cecilia Metella is certainly the most famous. This young patrician girl's tomb is in the style of an Etruscan tumulus and anticipates the great mauso-leums of Augustus and Hadrian. On a square stone base rises a cylindrical construction that encloses the small funeral chamber. The tomb, today decorated by Medieval crenelations, was surmounted by a pensile grove of cypresses.

There are many important monuments along the

Torre in Selce

Appian Way and in its surroundings: from the Baths of Caracalla to the Catacombs of St. Callisto and the several patrician tombs. The enormous, well-preserved Baths of Caracalla, today used for summer operatic performances, could accommodate some one thousand six hundred bathers and were built towards 212 AD by the Emperor Caracalla. It has gymnasiums, baths, music rooms and underground rooms. Except for a few traces of the old mosaic pavement, all the decorations have disappeared. Two famous ancient works were excavated here: the Farnese Hercules and the Farnese Taurus.

Catacombs of San Sebastiano, view of the three sepulchres   Catacombs of San Sebastiano, still-life with bird

THE ROMAN CATACOMBS

Etimologically the word "catacomba" derives from
Latin "ad catacumbas" (near the cavity).
The catacombs are underground burial-places, dug
by the first Christians between the 2nd and the 3rd
century to bury their deads and among them some
martyrs, too; their presence made the Catacombs
real veneration places and this import has remained unaltered during the centuries till now.
For a long time it has been believed that these underground places were the ones where the first
Christians hid to flee from persecutions. It has been
on the contrary proved by now they were not secret
places at all but well -known burial areas which were guarded by the Roman authorities of the time.
Only the scarcity of free spaces seems to be the reason why these first christian cemeteries were underground.
As well as other burial-places they were situated outside the city walls and along consular roads consti-
tuting another city, an underground ring which ex-
tends for hundreds of kilometres of galleries. The
subsoil, being above all formed by tuff, has caused

Catacombs of San Sebastiano, Bernini, bust of San Sebastiano

79

Catacombs of the San Callisto, Crypt of the Popes

Catacombs of San Callisto, unwalled tombs and fresco of five saints

Catacombs of Domitilla, Christ and the Apostles

Catacombs of Priscilla, central gallery on the first floor ▷

the development of such a burial method.

The most famous catacombs are those of San Sebastiano, Domitilla and San Callisto.

In the Catacombs of San Sebastiano, along the Appian Way, besides the crypt of San Sebastian several inscriptions and decorations with animals (symbols for the Christians of the time) can be admired.

The Catacombs of Domitilla are situated on Via delle Sette Chiese 282 near the above-mentioned old Appian Way.

The place where they have been dug seems to have been donated by the roman matron they have been dedicated to. Of particular interest are the Basilica of the Santi Martiri Nereo and Achilleo of the 4th century, the hypogeum of the Flavi and several frescoes with scenes from the New and Old Testament.

In the catacombs of San Callisto, situated on the old Appian Way, are the crypt of the Papi Martiri, dated back to the 3rd century, on which the homonymous saint, saint Urban and the face of Christ are represented.

The statue of Saint Cecily by Carlo Maderno and the cubicles of the Sacraments are particular interest.

Catacombs of Domitilla, tomb of Veneranda Arcosolio

Saint Peter's Basilica from Via della Conciliazione

Swiss Guards

THE VATICAN CITY

We now visit the Vatican City before we move on to important masterpieces and sacred memorials. It is the smallest state in the world (0,44 kilometres) and is located on the hill of the same name, between the hills Monte Mario and Monte Gianicolo.

Here, where the Emperor Caligula had built a circus and Saint Peter was martyred in 67 AD, rises the most important basilica in the Christian world.

The Vatican State was established during the Middle Ages and it grew to include most of central Italy. Wiped out by the Unification of Italy in 1870, the state was re-established in 1929 and ratified by the Lateran Treaty between the Holy See and the Italian State. The Vatican State has its own police, diplomatic corps and army, including the famous Swiss Guards. They were founded in 1505 by Julius II. Originally two hundred Swiss guards made up the Pope's personal guard. Their evocative uniforms, the design attributed to Michelangelo, have remained unchanged for five centuries.

Piazza San Pietro

Saint Peter's Square, the centre of Christianity for over a thousand years, is artistically and religiously moving.
It is a huge place, harmoniously open to the heavens, a perfect ellipse two hundred and forty metres wide, and surrounded by magnificent colonnades by Bernini.
It contains two hundred and eighty-four Doric pillars set in four rows and surmounted on the entablature by one hundred and forty statues of Saints and Martyrs.
There are two great fountains on each side by Maderno and at the centre, in 1586, an Egyptian

Obelisk was placed (a relic of the True Cross is kept on its summit).
There are two interesting things to look out for in this square: by standing between the two fountains, on a round porphyry slab, the two hundred and eighty four pillars seem set perfectly in a row and only the first column is visible; to the right of the basilica are the apostolic palaces, between which the Sistine Chapel is visible.
On its triangular shaped roof can be seen the famous chimney from which comes the white smoke announcing that a new Pope has been elected.

Saint Peter's Basilica

Here at one time was Nero's Circus, here St. Peter was martyred and the Apostles were buried. Because of this, Constantine, newly converted to Christianity, had built on this very spot a basilica around which Pope Symmachus in 500 AD built the first residence of the bishop of Rome.

Throughout the centuries the district grew in size. Here it was on Christmas Day (800 AD) that on the tomb of St. Peter, and not in the cathedral of Rome (which was then the church of S. Giovanni in Laterano), that Leo III crowned Charlemagne. In 1377 the exiled Popes retur-

ning from Avignon, established the Curia here until Julius II decided to build in the place of the old basilica of Constantine, now become unsafe, a new splendid church; the work was entrusted to the architect Bramante. The building of this church took more than a hundred and fifty years. On the death of Bramante in 1514, Raphael took over, followed by Antonio da Sangallo the Younger, who continued until 1546 when the task was finally passed on to Michelangelo, who decided on a church in the shape of a Greek cross and designed the dome, but he only saw it completed as far as the drum.

Later, Paul V entrusted Carlo Maderno to revert to the

POSTPAVLVS V BVRGHESIVS ROMANVS PONT MAX AN MDCXII PONT VII

Latin cross, to add three chapels on each side, and to build the façade; the latter was built between 1606 and 1614 but was criticised because too large in proportion to its height. In 1626 Bernini, certainly the greatest Baroque architect, was entrusted to reconstruct the façade; he had the superb idea of building an immense elliptical colonnade for the square.

The crowning feature of St. Peter's is the grandiose dome by Michelangelo visible from every part of the city. The dome stands on a drum which has a series of windows surmounted by elegant pediments, alternately semi-circular and triangular, separated by double columns. You get to the dome by climbing five hundred and thirty seven steps or by using the elevator: from the top you can enjoy a lovely view of Rome. The sphere that crowns the dome's lantern is so big it can hold a few people. In front of the façade is a portico by Maderno containing the *equestrian statues* of Constantine (by Bernini), the first Christian Emperor and Charlemagne (by Cornacchioni), the first Emperor of the Holy Roman Empire. Five doors lead into the basilica. The last door on the right is the Holy Door, only opened during the Holy Year, the middle door is the 4th century so-called Door of Filarete and the last door on the left is the recent Door of Death (1964) done by Giacomo Manzù for Pope John XXIII.

Nave

Inside the Basilica

Here we are in the sublime, harmonious vastness of the biggest Christian church. It is over two hundred and ten metres long and the dome is a hundred and thirty six metres high. A good idea of the vastness of it all is obtained by bearing in mind that the putti (baby angels) are bigger than a man, while the immense central canopy is as high as a Roman palace.

There are so many things to see, that we can but discuss the most important: the *Pietà* by Michelangelo, sculptured by the great artist (who was not yet twenty five years old), for the jubilee of 1500 AD. It is the only work

signed by the artist (his name is carved on the sash of the Madonna). This work of extraordinary beauty is totally different from the tragic Pietàs sculptured later by Michelangelo; in this one, for example, the Madonna is depicted, strangely enough, like a girl. Also important are: the bronze *Baldachin* by Bernini and the beautiful and venerated statue of St. Peter. The *Baldachin* is a gigantic baroque structure upheld by spiral pillars, cast using the bronze decorations from the Pantheon. It was placed over the papal high altar which is actually over the *Tomb of St. Peter* (1624-1633). The ninety nine lights of the hemycycle are kept permanently lit to illuminate the tomb of St. Peter. Years later Alexander VII entrusted

Statue of St. Peter

Michelangelo, Pietà

Bernini to redesign the apse. The artist conceived a reliquary *throne* in gilded bronze, large Baroque construction protecting the *wooden throne*, considered to be the true throne of St. Peter. Surmounted by a *bright glory of rays* and by the *dove of the Holy Spirit*, it is crowded by innumerable figures in gilded stucco. There are two great sepulchral monuments on each side: the *tomb of Pope Paul II* (1575, by Guglielmo della Porta) and the *Tomb of Pope Urban VIII* (1647, by Bernini). By the dome's *pillars* are four Statues of

Saints, amongst which St. Longinus by Bernini (in his hand is the spear that pierces the body of Christ). We conclude our visit with the Sacristy and the Museum of Saint Peter's Treasury, where we find a precious Ciborium by Donatello and the Tomb of Pope Sixtus IV by Antonio del Pollaiolo.

 Finally, we will visit the Caves of the Vatican (entrance from a pillar of the dome). Here, we find the remains of the ancient Costantinian Basilica and the tombs of many pontiffs.

The Laocoon group

Melozzo da Forlì, Musician Angel with viola

THE VATICAN MUSEUMS

The Vatican Palaces, enormous constructions with over 1400 rooms, host the precious Vatican Museums. A collection of antiquities, the most outstanding in the world, is gathered in the Pio Clementino Museum and the Chiaramonti Museum. However, the great Italian and European collection of paintings is kept in the eighteen rooms of the Vatican Picture-Gallery built by Luca Beltrami for Pope Pius XI.

In the ancient Roman Museum, enriched by Julius II in the 16th century, there are many works of art, among which the Laocoon. It represents the Trojan priest with his two sons being crushed to death by snakes as a penalty for warning the Trojans against the wooden horse. Of uncertain date - it may be a Hellenistic sculpture - it was found in 1506 in the "Domus Aurea". It depicts human pain and moral suffering with great

pathos. The admirable *Belvedere Torso*, perhaps representing Hercules, was sculptured at the end of the 1st century BC. It was found in the 15th century and was studied extensively by Michelangelo. The Apollo of Belvedere is a Roman copy of a Greek work of art from the 4th century BC. Other works of art are the *Augustus of the Prima Porta*, a Roman statue. Especially admirable are the bas-relief of the cuirass and the *Sleeping Ariadne*, where Ariadne, abandoned by Thesius, sleeps in an affected pose. The drapery is typical of Hellenistic sculpture, of which this is a Roman copy.

Do not miss the *Wounded Amazon* (a copy of Phidias, 500 BC) and the *Apoxyomenos* (athlete scraping himself with a strigil), an original bronze by Lysippus, and the *Doryphorus* (spear carrier) a copy by Polycletus.

In the Vatican Picture-Gallery the development of art can be followed through the centuries. Beginning with the *Stefaneschi polyptych* by Giotto (1300 AD), the

Caravaggio, Deposition

Raffaello, Transfiguration

Raphael, Madonna of Foligno

Leonardo, Saint Jerome

splendid *Musician Angel* by Melozzo da Forlì (a golden halo, lapis-lazuli sky) and, by the same artist, *Sixtus IV and Platina*. The latter is a fresco where the Pope and his nephew (the future Julius II) stand with the Humanist called Platina. Admirable are: the *Madonna and Child* by Pinturicchio and the St. Benedict by Perugino (1495). By Raphael are the admirable: *Madonna of Foligno*, commissioned as a thanks offering to the Virgin, one of Raphael's first works comple-

ted in Rome in 1512, and the *Transfiguration* where Christ, bathed in supernatural light, arises supported by Moses and the prophet Elijah, while the apostles lie terrorised on the ground. This admirable work was given new splendour after its recent restoration. The museum also hosts the unfinished but beautiful *Saint Jerome* by Leonardo, the *Pietà* by Giovanni Bellini and works of art of Van Dyck , Pietro da Cortona, Poussin, Titian and the splendid *Deposition* (1604) by Caravaggio.

Stanza dell'incendio di Borgo

Raphael's Rooms

In 1508 Pope Julius II wanted to finish the decorations of his apartments, started by Signorelli and Piero della Francesca but interrupted shortly after. Therefore, he entrusted to Raphael, a young artist whose genius has been compared to that of Leonardo and Michelangelo, with the work.

The most beautiful room painted by Raphael is, perhaps, the *Stanza della Segnatura*, based on a complex programme in which theological, philosophical and political ideas are expressed through allegories. This is how the *Disputation over the Sacraments* was conceived, a great religious and symbolic fresco. *The Parnassus* is a fresco where Apollo is playing a violin among the Muses (here represented for the first time

since antiquity) and a crowd of poets such as Alcaeus, Corinna, Petrarch, Anacreon, Ennius and the lonely Sappho (the only one not wearing a laurel wreath) as well as a group with Dante, Homer, Virgil and on the other side more poets: Pindar, Sannazzaro, Horace, Propertius, Tibullus, Catullus, Ovid and at the centre Ariosto. It is a great fresco celebrating poetry and beauty. Splendid, and probably the best known painting, is the so-called *School of Athens* an allegory of ancient philosophy as anticipator of Christianity. Then, the *Stanza dell'Incendio*, so-called because it depicts Pope Leo IV miraculously putting out a fire. Lastly, the *Stanza di Costantino* and the *Stanza di Eliodoro* of which the last painting is the *Expulsion of Eliodorus from the Temple* (standing to one side of the papal throne, dressed in a long black robe is Raphael - a self-portrait).

THE RESTORATION OF THE SISTINE CHAPEL FRESCOES

The restoration of Michelangelo's frescoes in the Sistine Chapel represents the natural sequel to the work carried out between 1964 and 1974 on the fifteenth century *Histories of Moses and of Christ* on the side walls, and again between 1979 and 1980 on the sixteenth century repainting of the two biblical episodes on the entrance wall.

The cleaning of Michelangelo's ceiling was to have followed that of the series of portraits of the Popes, but the conditions noted in the lunette of *Eleazar Mathan* - in particular the presence of numerous micro-tears in the painted surface - advised against further delay, and between 1980 and 1984 the fourteen lunettes with the *Ancestor of Christ* were cleaned, together with the *Popes* by Perugino, Ghirlandaio, Botticelli and Cosimo Rosselli.

The damage proved to be the result of variations in temperature and humidity, causing contractions in the layer of glue which during past restorations had been applied to the painted surface as a varnish in order to revive the colours, darkened and dulled by the gradual build-up of deposits of dust and candle-black that the methods of cleaning generally used - bread, sour wine and water - were not able to sufficiently lighten. The restoration revealed a pure colour, fully of iridescent effects, and very similar to that brought to light by the careful restoration of the *Doni Tondo*, also being carried out at that time. And yet it was unexpected, and consequently raised doubts and incredulity in some critics, causing the fierce polemic that for a time accompanied the work. Following this first period of work, the cleaning of the ceiling itself took place between 1985 and 1989 and confirmed the results of the restoration of the lunettes.

Finally, from the spring of 1990, work went ahead on the *Last Judgement*, revealing yet again a rich source of new knowledge.

As we know, every restoration provides a rich and almost inexhaustible source of information about the functioning of the creative process and gives clues and solutions to problems of dating, iconography and style relating to the creation of the work of art.

If this is true in general, it is all the more so in the case of Michelagelo's frescoes, where the smoke, dust, dirt and restorations of nearly five centuries had deposited a patina, which, if not noble, was undoubtedly suggestive, giving rise to the myth of an artist who technically lacked preparation. The cleaning of the ceiling has, however, revealed the work of a typical Renaissance artist, a sculptor by vocation, a reluctant painter and architect, with a technical background and artistic preparation that enabled him, despite his apparent inexperience, to tackle the most monumental challenge that an artist had ever faced, creating a work of exceptional skill both in terms of formal perfection and of technical achievement, the equivalent of a treatise on mural painting.

True to his Florentine origins, Michelangelo painted in *buon fresco*, gradually eliminating from his palette - perhaps because of problems of 'mould' in the early stages - those colours like red lead that required the use of a binding medium.

The use of *fresco secco* was limited to retouching and to the monochrome medallions at the feet of the *Ignudi*. From the point of view of technique of execution, all the methods employed - in particular the use of enamel and lapislazuli in fresco - came from the workshop of Domenico Ghirlandaio, where Michelangelo served his apprenticeship, and from where he summoned most of the assistants who worked with him in the early stages of the work: Bugiardini, Jacopo di Sandro - with whom he immediately came into conflict - Jacopo di Lazzaro Torni known as Indaco

Vecchio, who took the latter'place in January 1509, and his childhood friend, Granacci, who had introduced him to the bottega of Ghirlandaio.

Michelangelo could certainly not have learnt, during the brief stay of these 'assistants' on the scaffolding, the difficult technique of painting in true fresco; they helded to 'freshen up' the knowledge assimilated during his apprenticeship with Ghirlandaio. They assisted in the layout of the work and painted not only the decorative elements of the cornices but also - under the rigid and constant control of the master - some of the figures of the stories of Noah. We note their presence in the different modes of painting and, often, in the sudden lowering of quality compared to the parts by Michelangelo which, even in the early stages, are of a constantly high level, unattainable by any other artist.

The assistants worked with him until the autumn of 1509 when the scale of the figures and the rhythms of the composition in the *Fall of Man* made it impossible for them to work with him on the scaffolding in any way that was even partially autonomous. So Michelangelo sent home the more able of his assistants - Granacci and Bugiardini in particular - above all because, according to the contract, all the expenses fell to him and there was no sense in keeping them if he could not put them to good use.

The decoration has also substantiated the fact, indicated by the chronicles and letters, that there was a pause in the work in the summer of 1510, immediately after Michelangelo had painted the *Creation of Eve*, below which stood significantly the marble screen separating the laity from the clergy. It has also shown that once work started again in the autumn of 1511, the pace accelerated remarkably, so that, for example, the lunette of *Rehoboam and Abjijah* and the scene of the *Separation of light from darkness* were painted in one day. One reason for this acceleration was probably the use, in the scenes from Genesis in the centre of the ceiling and of the groups of figures in the spandrels, of the indirect impression, dispensing with the pouncing of the *spolvero* as used almost everywhere in the first series of frescoes.

As a result of the cleaning, the influence that Michelangelo had on his contemporaries becomes more than evident. It can be seen in Raphael and his entourage - particulary Giulio Romano - as well as in the so-called Florentine Mannerism of Rosso, Pontormo, Andrea del Sarto and Beccafumi, who were influenced not only in formal terms but also - and this was not noted before - by his use of colour.

It was a very different artist who painted the Last Judgement little more than twenty years later. Technically Michelangelo executed his composition in *buon fresco* as before on the ceiling, but here his palette is richer and, alongside the usual earth colours, we find pigments such as red lake, *giallolino* and orpiment. For the blue of the sky he freely used the very expensive lapis-lazuli, most probably chosen because here it was longer the artist who bore the expense but the Pope.

Apart from this detail the use of is lapis-lazuli fundamental, for it determines the generally much warmer tone, clearly a result of the artist's changing sensibility, influenced undoubtedly both by his familiarity over a period of twenty years with the work of Sebastiano del Piombo and by a journey to Venice made in 1529.

Althoug essentially Florentine by training, Michelangelo turned in his later works to new ideas that in terms of light and colour came from the Venetian School, showing his awareness of the outside world and his lack of prejudice towards a cultural environment about which, in words at least, he expressed many reservations.

Fabrizio Mancinelli.

(From the volume: "Michelangelo, painter, sculptor, architect") Edizione ATS Italia Editrice - F.Papafava Editore

Michelangelo, Vault of the Sistine Chapel, Creation of Adam

Vault of the Sistine Chapel, Expulsion from Paradise

The Sistine Chapel

The Chapel (40,5 metres long, 20,7 metres high and 13,20 metres wide) was built at the end of the 15th century by Giovanni Dolci.

The walls were frescoed with twelve paintings (on the left scenes from the *Life of Moses*, on the right scenes from the *Life of Jesus*) by such artists as: Perugino, Pinturicchio, Botticelli, Signorelli and Ghirlandaio. However the greatest masterpieces of them all remain the frescoes of the vaults, painted by Michelangelo for Pope Julius II between 1508 and 1512 and the admirable and terrible *Last Judgement* painted for Pope Paul III around 1540.

Admirable are the decorative figures and biblical scenes which crowd the frescoes of the vault, a gigantic work that Michelangelo executed alone and in an extremely uncomfortable position. Powerful

Michelangelo, Vault of the Sistine Chapel, Prophet Ezechiel, detail

Michelangelo, Vault of the Sistine Chapel, Profeta Gioele, detail

Michelangelo, Vault of the Sistine Chapel, Delphic Sibyl, detail

Michelangelo, Last Judgment

nude figures, assuming a variety of poses, separate and frame the paintings that contain scenes developing the great iconographic theme that goes from Creation and Original Sin to Redemption.

In the *Creation of Adam* the divine finger is almost united to that of the first man in whom God instils life.

Admirable are: *God separating light from darkness, The creation of the sun and the moon, The separation of earth and water, The creation of Eve, Original sin*, and the well-known and dramatic *Expulsion from Paradise, The story of Cain and Abel*, The *Flood*, The *drunkenness of Noah*.

The powerful figures of the seven prophets and of the five sibyls frame the sides of this grandiose work of art. Perhaps even more famous is the huge outstanding *Last Judgment* on the altar wall.

The scene is unique, made up of three hundred and ninety one figures surrounding Christ the Judge: near and above Him are the elect who rise at the sound of the trumpets, while below the damned are being led to hell by Charon and Minos.

Almost all the figures are naked and of great beauty while the whole is composed of hundreds of expressive scenes that circulate like a vortex, at once solemn and arresting.

Rarely before has a work of art been able to express Man's dramatic destiny with such intensity.

Gallery of the Geographical Maps

Danti, Ancient Italy

... the visit goes on

The visit to the Vatican Palaces has other surprises in store: the Gallery of the Geographical Maps, the Gallery of the Tapestries, the Gallery of the Candelabras and The Hall of the Biga (because it exhibits a biga from the 1st century BC).

Façade

Central nave

San Giovanni in Laterano

The Basilica of San Giovanni in Laterano is perhaps the most ancient of Christian churches. It is held to be the most important after Saint Peter's, because it is the Cathedral of Rome. In the central space between the transepts is an altar where only the Pope, the bishop of Rome, can celebrate mass. As in all major basilicas, the entrance is preceded by a large portico; here is placed a statue of Constantine. The basilica has five doors; the one on the extreme right can only be opened during Holy Year, like that one in Saint Peter's. The façade of

Apse

San Giovanni in Laterano is a masterpiece by Alessandro Galilei (1732) showing strong influences of the Baroque and Neo-classicism. Fifteen colossal statues crown the façade, the most conspicuous being that of Christ.

The evocative and beautiful interior has five naves built in 1650 by Francesco Borromini. The *transept* is earlier and contains a beautiful *tabernacle* by Giovanni di Stefano. The left side of the transept leads to the extraordinary Cloister, a true masterpiece of the 13th century by the Vassalletto family. Very close to the church is an antique Baptistery commissioned by Constantine at the same time as the basilica; it is octagonal and in the centre is a green basalt urn, once a baptismal font.

Façade

Central nave, Canopy

Santa Maria Maggiore

This grandiose church stands on the Esquiline Hill. It was built under the pontificate of Sixtus III in the early 15th century and its Romanesque bell tower is the highest in Rome (75 metres).

The mid-18th century façade has five arches and a loggia by Ferdinando Fuga (in the loggia lovely *mo-saics* from a previous façade).

Inside there are three naves, a beautiful pavement with geometric designs, and a *coffered ceiling* by Giuliano da Sangallo. Along the central nave are thirty six mosaic panels depicting *scenes from the Old Testament*.

The mosaics over the *Triumphal Arch*, which represent scenes from the *Life of Jesus* and *the Virgin*

MARIA · VIRGO · ASSVPTA·E· AD·ETHEREV·THALAMV· IN·Q·VO·REX·REGV· STELLATO·SEDET·SOLIO·
EXALTATA·GS·T· SANCTA·DEI·GENITRIX· SVPER·CHOROS·ANGELORVM· AD·CELESTIA·REGNA·

Apsidal mosaic

Sistin Chapel, inside

and those over the apse by Jacopo Torriti (1295 with the triumph of Maria) are beautiful. These mosaics, which span several centuries, are amongst the most precious and beautiful in existence. Noteworthy are also the chapels of this basilica: the Sistine Chapel (built by Domenico Fontana for Pope Sixtus V) and the Paolina Chapel (built by Flaminio Ponzi for Pope Paul V).

Façade

Central Nave

San Paolo Fuori le Mura

One hundred and thirty metres long and 65 metres wide, this is the second largest basilica in Rome after St. Peter's. Started under the reign of Constantine, it was completed in 395 AD.

Over the centuries it was enriched with paintings and frescoes until in July 823 AD a terrible fire almost burnt it to the ground. The basilica was rebuilt in 1928 following the original design (including the portico in front of the façade, called "of the hundred columns"). Inside there are many works of art: the Byzantine-Venetian *mosaics in the apse*, the Gothic *Ciborium* by Arnolfo di Cambio, in the *Chapel of the Holy*

Cloister

Detail of the column

Sacrament the *mosaic* representing the Holy Virgin, the frieze with mosaic portraits of the Popes, the *Triumphal Arch* at the far end of the central nave, the *Byzantine bronze panels* of the *Holy Door*, and the harmonious cloister with *multicoloured marbles*, *mosaics* and smooth and spiral-shaped *columns*.

Michelangelo, Grave of Pope Julius II

San Pietro in Vincoli

This very old church, dedicated to the Apostles, was erected in the 5ᵗʰ century and completely renovated by Pope Julius II at the end of the 15ᵗʰ century.

It owes its name to the relic it contains ("in vincoli", "enchained"), namely the chains that bound St. Peter in Jerusalem and later in Rome (they are kept in a gilded bronze urn). The other great attraction of the church is the *Mausoleum of Julius II*, an unfinished work by Michelangelo. He worked on it from 1513 to 1516 and it was originally destined to stand in St. Peter's. For the mausoleum he sculpted the famous *Statue of Moses* and the two Prisoners, now in the Louvre.

Façade Apsidal Mosaic ▷

Santa Maria in Trastevere

The first church to be dedicated to the Madonna, and amongst the oldest in Rome, has undergone many chan-

ges: from the foundation dating from around 340 AD until the recent restorations of the 19th century - not very good. The church has three naves and assumed its present aspect under Pope Innocent II who had the sanctuary re-

Cavallini Pietro, *Birth of Mary*

constructed in the 12th century, ornamenting the apse with splendid *mosaics*, under Byzantine influence. These mo-saics represent on the triumphal arch the *Prophets, Symbols of the Evangelists*, the branched candlestick of the

136

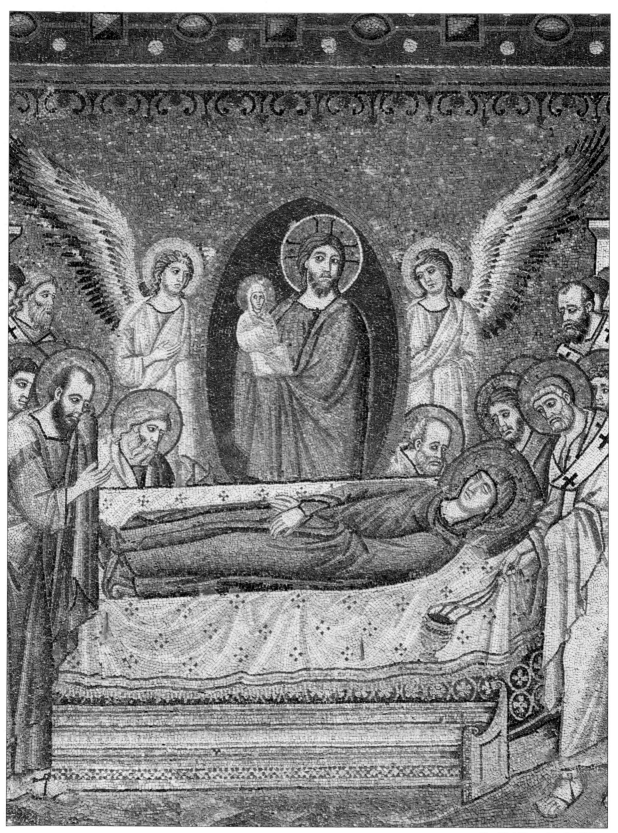

Cavallini Pietro, Death of Mary

Apocalypse, and the *Cross*. In the semicircular recess of the apse is the extremely beautiful *mosaic of Christ crowning* *the Virgin*; beneath the *mosaics, the cycle of the life of Mary* by Pietro Cavallini, at the end of the 13th century.

Façade

Mouth of Truth

Santa Maria in Cosmedin

Built in the 4th century, this church was also constructed on an ancient Roman building and takes its name from the Greek word meaning "embellished".

Beneath the portico in front of the façade, is the Mouth of Truth, an ancient lid in the shape of a mask.

According to legend any liar who puts his hand into the slit will have it snapped off.

Although the church has no masterpieces, it is rich in interesting objects: the elegant Romanesque bell tower, the richly decorated pavements and the Gothic canopy protecting the main altar. Visit the *Crypt* dug in tuff, perhaps the remains of an antique pagan altar.

Santa Maria in Aracoeli, Façade

Santa Maria in Aracoeli

The church was begun in the 14th century by the Franciscans, while the marble staircase - a votive offering for a deliverance from the plague - was added in the middle of the same century. Inside there are three naves.

Noteworthy the lovely *pavement*, by the Cosmati and the richly decorated *wooden coffered ceiling* (in the middle the *Virgin with Child*).

Here are one of the most loved and venerated images of the Romans (in the left transept): the *statue of the Holy Child* which is said to have been sculpted from an olive tree from Gethsemane and which is held to be miraculous. Noteworthy are the *Stories of San Bernardino*, a 15th century masterpiece by Pinturicchio.

Over the main altar is the wooden panel depicting a *Madonna with Child* (a work dating from around 1000 AD), to whom is dedicated the grandiose staircase in front of the church.

Statue of the Holy Child

San Clemente, Schola Cantorum

San Clemente

Few basilicas are of so many different styles and have been added to as frequently, as the Basilica of St. Clement. The original early-Christian basilica was built on a pre-existing Roman building of the time of Domitian (the remains can be visited) dating from the end of the 4th century and dedicated to the third Pope, Clement. At the beginning of the 13th century, the actual basilica was built over the old one, which was discovered during excavations at the end of the last century. The façade of the Basilica is preceded by an atrium and a pronaos, whilst in the middle of the central nave is a Schola Cantorum. The *mosaic* that covers the apse is magnificent and represents the *Triumph of the Cross*. Very lovely are the 15th century frescoes by Masolino di Panicale in the Chapel of St. Catherine. The early Medieval frescoes are extremely interesting

and form a complete cycle dedicated to St. Clement and others illustrating the *Legend of Sisinius* that can be visited in the *lower basilica*.

Sant'Andrea della Valle

This church is noteworthy for its beautiful dome (a 17th century work by Maderno on an octagonal drum) the highest in Rome after St. Peter's. The church was built at the end of the 16th century by Pietro Paolo Olivieri and the aforementioned Maderno. The façade, however, is from the mid-17th century, and was built by Rainaldi and Fontana. The fresco decorating the vault of the dome represents the Glory of Paradise by Lanfranco, and in the curve of the apse are three frescoes by Mattia Preti (1540) telling the story of the Martyrdom of St. Andrew. From St. Peter's come the two tombs of Popes Pius II and III, both members of the Piccolomini family.

SURROUNDINGS

Old Ostia

Ostia Antica, panorama

Old Ostia

Far from the noise of the city, in the peace of the surrounding countryside, among the pine trees, heralds of the sea Rome has many superb walks, the first one being in old Ostia. Of the antique Roman port, built in the 4th century BC, there still remain houses, taverns, patrician villas, temples and fountains which stand amidst lush vegetation.

Old Ostia

The most notable excavations are the Mithraeum, the Egyptian temples and the synagogue. Not to be missed is the Museo Ostiense. In the beautiful Theatre of Augustus famous classical performances are held during the summer. You can go down the Tiber by boat from here to Rome: a picturesque and nostalgic journey.

Tivoli, Hadrian Villa, Poikile

Tivoli, Hadrian Villa, Canopus

Tivoli

Tivoli is situated on the banks of the river Aniene near the famous falls where Roman patricians used to build their summer residences. Here is the famous Hadrian Villa, the largest and richest ancient Roman villa built after 100 AD.

The complex contains the lyceum the Academy, the Poikile (a rectangular peristyle with a central fish-pond), the Canopus (a long narrow basin built in

Villa d'Este, Fountain of Neptune

Villa d'Este, Hundred small fountains

a natural hollow). The Villa d'Este and the Villa Gregoriana date from the Renaissance period.
The former, built by Pirro Ligorio in 1550 for Cardinal Ippolito II of Este, stands in the famous park decorated by delightful fountains and small cascades. Near the

Villa Gregoriana are the famous Cascades of the river Aniene which flow down picturesquely amid a rocky landscape. This spot inspired the great writer Marguerite Yourcenar to write her famous novel *Hadrian's Memoirs*.

Castel Gandolfo, view

Castel Gandolfo ▷

Roman Castles

A visit to the picturesque towns known as Castelli Romani (Roman Castles) makes a delightful Sunday outing. Located south of Rome they are renowned for their excellent food and wine. In Frascati, of great interest is Villa Aldobrandini, whose immense façade gives onto a luxuriant park. Villa Falconieri is also very beautiful but can be visited only on request. Worth a visit is also the interesting Abbazia di Grottaferrata, an abbey built around 1000 AD. Not to be missed is Castel Gandolfo, the Pope's summer residence. Our visit ends with the town of Palestrina, famous for the ruins of the old city walls and for the huge Sanctuary of Fortune.

The Vatican City

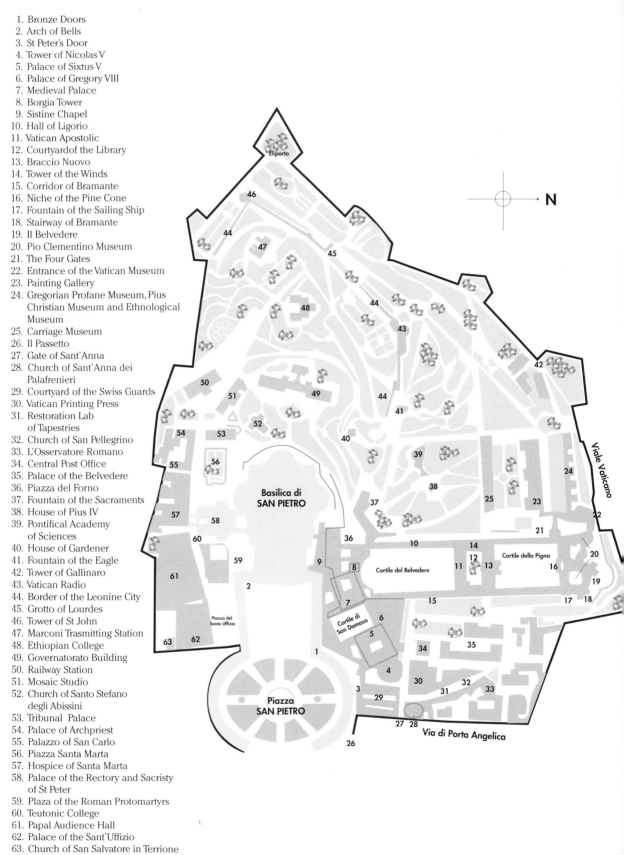

Plan of St. Peter's Basilica

1. Portico or Atrium
2. Holy Door
3. Center Door
4. Door of Good and Evil
5. Door of Death
6. Interior
7. Pietà by Michelangelo
8. Monument to Pius XII
9. Chapel of the Blessed Sacrament
10. Monument to Gregory XIII
11. Gregorian Chapel
12. Statue of St. Peter
13. Baldachin by Bernini
14. Altar of the Confession
15. Tomb of St. Peter
16. The four Relics
17. The Dome
18. The Right Transept
19. Monument to Pope Clement XIII
20. Chapel of St. Petronilla
21. Chapel of the Cathedra
22. Monument to Pope Urban VIII
23. Monument to Pope Paul III
24. Chapel of St. Leo the Great
25. Madonna of the Column
26. Monument to Pope Alexander VII
27. Left Transept
28. Chapel of St. Gregory the Great
29. Monument to Pope Pius VII
30. Chapel of the Transfiguration
31. Choir Chapel
32. Monument to Pope Innocent VIII
33. Monument to Pope John XXIII
34. Chapel of St. Pius X
35. Monument to Pope Benedict XV
36. Stuart Monument
37. Baptistry Chapel

This volume has been edited and realized by:
Ats Italia Editrice srl
Via di Brava, 41-43 - 00163 Roma
tel. 0666415961 · fax 0666512461
www.atsitalia.it

Text
Pier Francesco Listri from the volume
"Venice Florence Naples Rome and the Vatican City"
edited by Ats Italia Editrice - Editrice Giusti - Kina Italia

The text "The Roman Catacomba" (pages 79 and 82)
edited by Fratel Arno

Editing and technical coordination
Frida Giannini
Graphics, impagination and book - cover
Ats Italia Editrice (Sabrina Moroni - Roberta Belli)
Photolithography
Gamba srl, Rome - Scriba srl, Florence
Printing
Papergraf srl, Piazzola sul Brenta (PD)
Photography
Archivio Ats Italia Editrice
(G. Cozzi - M. Borchi - D. Busi - F. Borra - G.Bocchieri - M. Cirilli - M.Grassi
L.Giordano - M.Amantini - A. Regoli - G. Galazka - C. Tini - L. Marinelli)
Archivio Fotografico della Fabbrica di San Pietro
Archivio Fotografico Musei Vaticani
Archivio Scala
K&B News Foto - Buonafede

The publisher is at the disposal of the party entlited as regards
iconographical sources not identified

Creazione di Adamo
Michelangelo, Cappella Sistina

Scuola di Atene
Raffaello, Stanza della Segnatura

San Matteo e l'angelo
Guido Reni, Pinacoteca

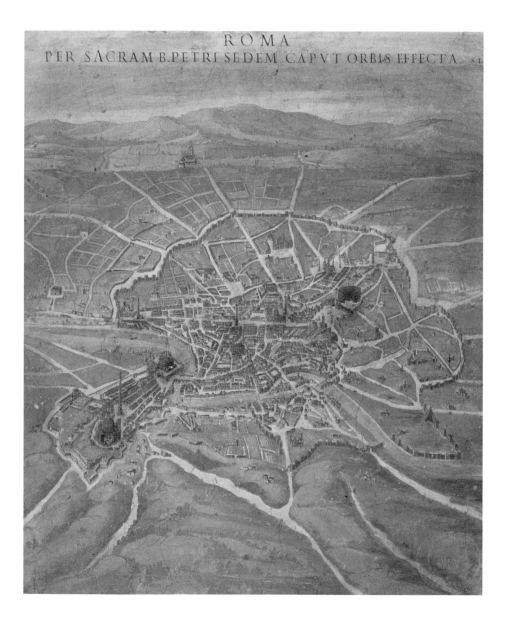

Pianta di Roma
Ignazio Danti, Galleria delle Carte Geografiche